CITIES AT WAR

LENINGRAD
★ ★ ★

Trudy J. Hanmer

new
Discovery
B·O·O·K·S

New York

Maxwell Macmillan Canada
Toronto

Maxwell Macmillan International
New York   Oxford   Singapore   Sydney

For Fantasia

Front Cover Photo: Tass from Sovfoto
Back Cover Photo: Sovfoto
Interior Photos:
  Sovfoto: 4, 19, 30, 34, 36-37, 40, 42, 43, 45, 46, 48, 50, 54, 57, 60,
    63, 70, 72-73, 75, 76-77, 78, 80, 83, 84, 85, 87
  Tass from Sovfoto: 8, 14-15, 17, 22, 24, 25, 26, 29, 64-65, 66, 69, 91
  Sovfoto from Artkino: 10, 59
  Novosti from Sovfoto: 12, 20, 39, 53, 88
Map on pages 6-7: Kathie Kelleher

New Discovery Books
Macmillan Publishing Company
866 Third Avenue
New York, NY 10022

Maxwell Macmillan Canada, Inc.
1200 Eglinton Avenue East
Suite 200
Don Mills, Ontario M3C 3N1

Macmillan Publishing Company is part of the Maxwell Communication
Group of Companies.

First Edition

Printed in the United States of America

10 9 8 7 6 5 4 3 2 1

Library of Congress Cataloging-in-Publication Data

Hanmer, Trudy J.
    Leningrad / by Trudy J. Hanmer.
        p.   cm. — (Cities at War).
    Includes bibliographical references.
    Summary: Describes life in the Russian city of Leningrad during
World War II.
    ISBN 0-02-742616-7
    1. Leningrad (R.S.F.S.R.)—History—Siege, 1941–1944—Juvenile
literature.   [1. Leningrad (R.S.F.S.R.)—History—Siege, 1941–1944.
2. World War. 1939–1945—Russian S.F.S.R.—Leningrad.]
I. Title. II. Series.
D764.3.L4H36   1992
947' .45—dc20   92–14

CONTENTS

★ ★ ★

Bundled up against the bitter cold, a woman listens to the radio for news during the siege.

1

BUT TWO NO LONGER BREATHE

In Leningrad in January the sun sets by three o'clock in the afternoon. Winter days in this northern Russian city are always cold, dark, and short. None ever seemed colder, darker, or shorter than the grim days of the winter of 1941–1942. For this was the first winter of a terrible stretch of time known as the Siege of Leningrad, as the city was then called. As part of his plan for world conquest, Adolf Hitler had turned the German army loose on the Soviet Union in July 1941. The Eastern Front, as the Soviet-German conflict was called, would become a critical area of World War II.

In Leningrad during the first winter of the war, the sounds of German gunfire rattled in the streets. Those doctors and health officials who had not been weakened too badly by the hunger that gripped Leningrad's citizens walked from house to house, trying to care for people too feeble to reach breadlines or hospitals. Some of the survivors of these efforts kept diaries or penned official reports detailing the horrors of the city under siege.

One such survivor, a woman named A. N. Mironova, wrote in her diary on a January evening that as she entered an apartment, "My eyes met a frightful sight. A half-dark room. Frost on the walls. On the floor a frozen puddle. On a chair the corpse of a 14-year-old boy. In a child's cradle the second corpse of a tiny child. On the bed

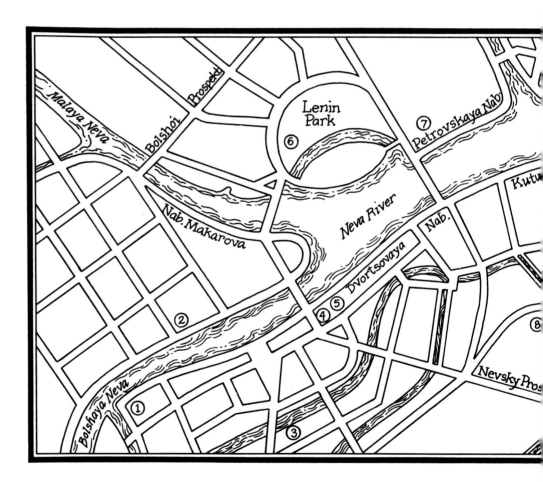

the dead mistress of the flat. Beside her rubbing the dead woman's breast with a towel, stood her oldest daughter, Mikki. In one day Mikki lost her mother, her son and her brother, all dead of hunger and cold."[1] Nor was Mikki's family alone in its plight. All over Leningrad people witnessed horrible scenes of death from starvation and cold.

A. N. Mironova was later awarded a city medal for her heroism in rescuing children during the siege. In another journal entry she wrote of finding a nine-year-old boy, Yuri Stepanov, who had

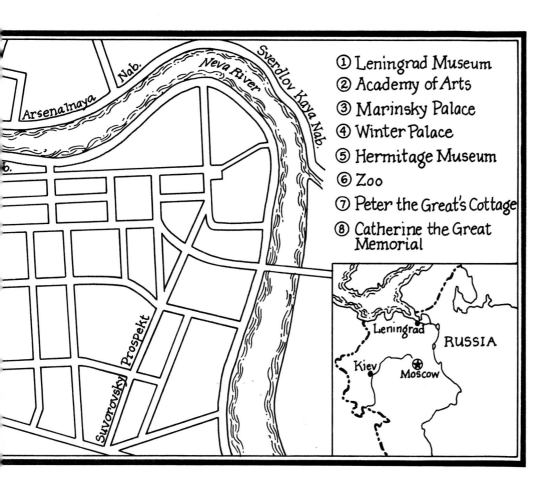

① Leningrad Museum
② Academy of Arts
③ Marinsky Palace
④ Winter Palace
⑤ Hermitage Museum
⑥ Zoo
⑦ Peter the Great's Cottage
⑧ Catherine the Great Memorial

A grim memorial to those who died during the siege: pages from Tanya's diary.

curled up by the body of his dead mother, too dazed from hunger to know that human warmth had passed from her forever. "How cold I got from Mama," he said in wonderment to his rescuer, because all through the heatless winter she had been his source of warmth in the night.[2] In another apartment, an 11-year-old girl was the only survivor in her family. Mironova described her: "Little girl dirty, scabs on her hands. Found her in a pile of dirty linen under the mattress."[3]

The story of another 11-year-old-girl is perhaps the most famous of the countless tales of death during the siege. Today in the Museum of the History of the City of Leningrad, visitors can view pages torn from a school notebook on which Tanya Savichev recorded the slow, painful obliteration of her family from cold and hunger. In disciplined Russian schoolgirl fashion, Tanya used the appropriate alphabetic file guide to record each loss:

Z — Zhenya died 28 December, 12:30 in the A.M., 1941
B — Babushka [Grandma] died 25 January, 3 o'clock, 1942
L — Leka died 17 March, 5 o'clock in the A.M., 1942
D — Dedya [Grandpa] Vasya, died 12 April, 2 o'clock at night, 1942
D — Dedya Lesha, died 10 May, 4 in the afternoon, 1942
M — Mama, died 13 May, 7:30 in the A.M., 1942
S — Savichevs died. All died. Only Tanya remains.[4]

Somehow Tanya survived the worst—and most terrible—winter of the siege. When the authorities discovered her alone in her family's apartment, they sent her to a children's home outside Leningrad. Sadly, the damage done to her young body during the winter of famine was irreparable. She died at the home in 1943.

Tanya and her family, Mikki's relatives, and the mother of Yuri Stepanov composed a tiny fraction of the hundreds of thou-

A broken water main supplies fresh water for citizens of Leningrad.

sands of people who died in the Siege of Leningrad. No family was untouched by death or hunger. One poet wrote about surviving as family members died around her: "There are three of us in the room, but two no longer breathe. They are dead."[5]

All the dead were victims of a cruel military scheme hatched in the mind of Adolf Hitler, the leader of Nazi Germany. For Hitler it was not enough to conquer the Soviet Union. In the winter of 1941–1942, German armies were ordered to surround Leningrad. Hitler planned, once the city was surrounded, to starve Leningrad's millions of citizens. By January 1942, there was almost no electricity, no running water, no fuel for heat, and not nearly enough food to feed the city's people. To most observers it seemed as though Hitler's plan would succeed.

The German leader had calculated the stores of grain, reserves of fuel, and size of the Russian army. What he had not figured on was the fiery spirit of the citizens of Leningrad. To those who lived there, the city held a unique place in their hearts and in their sense of Russian history. To starve was preferable to surrendering "Peter's City" to the hated enemy. As long as a crust of bread remained, the Leningraders would hold out. It would take nearly 900 days, but in the end their invincible spirit would overcome German military power.

The beautiful summer palace of Catherine II

2

WINDOW ON THE WEST

According to Russian legend, the city known as Leningrad was constructed in heaven and lowered in one piece onto the land at the mouth of the Neva River. As Peter the Great's biographer has written, "The truth is only slightly less miraculous."[1]

Long before there was a city called Leningrad, there was a city called St. Petersburg. And before there was a city called St. Petersburg, there was a vast, dismal swamp in the cold reaches of northern Russia, spread over the mouth of the Neva River between the banks of Lake Ladoga on the east and the shores of the Baltic Sea on the west. For centuries the region saw few human visitors except occasional sailors or peasant woodsmen. It took the will and vision of one of the most powerful czars in Russian history, Peter the Great, to build a magnificent city from the foggy marsh.

Early in Peter's life, he became convinced that Russia's capi-

tal city, Moscow, was too isolated and backward. Peter wanted Russia to share in the political power and culture of 17th-century Europe. He wanted Russia to become more westernized. The citizens of Moscow resisted Peter's efforts to westernize them, so Peter decided to move the Russian capital. He dreamed of a new city that

Decembrist Square in a peaceful moment before the onset of World War II.

would provide a "window on the west" for Russia. It would be located at the mouth of the Neva River, the longest river in Europe, and would face the Baltic Sea through the Gulf of Finland.

In 1703, Peter stood on the banks of the Neva and explained his plans to his architects and engineers. Less than ten years later—

15

in spite of war, material shortages, forced relocation, and resistance from the nobility—Peter declared St. Petersburg to be the capital of the Russian Empire. The city he called "paradise" and "heaven"[2] became the imperial city. The czars would live there, and for himself and his heirs, Peter commissioned the largest residence of all, the Winter Palace.

Together with the adjoining Hermitage, the Winter Palace became the largest royal residence in the world. The formal reception rooms with their inlaid parquet floors could hold thousands of people. As the main residence of the czar, the Winter Palace rivaled the palaces of the monarchs of England and France and the castles in the German and Austro-Hungarian empires. By the czar's decree, only church spires could rise higher than the roof of the Winter Palace, which was 92 feet (28 meters) tall. The French writer Voltaire said that "the united magnificence of all the cities of Europe could but equal St. Petersburg."[3] As admiration for the city grew and trade with the city brought prosperity, the royal court also learned to love St. Petersburg.

Great balls took place at court. Feasts of local delicacies, such as bear hams and elk fillets, were accompanied by grapes and citrus fruits brought at great expense from the Mediterranean. The czars spared no expense in stocking their wine cellars and liquor cabinets. Nor was fashion overlooked. The czarinas and other women of the court imported the latest French fashions in great quantity. When Catherine I died, her closets were found to hold tens of thousands of dresses.

For the common citizens of St. Petersburg, life was not so grand. The czars were harsh rulers. An unjust criminal process, heavy taxes, and mandatory military service made life difficult for everyday citizens who did not share in the glamour of the court. Yet

The famous statue of Peter the Great commissioned by Catherine the Great in 1792.

even the poorest citizens of Peter, as they affectionately called their city, were proud of their hometown.

In 1792 Catherine the Great commissioned a statue of Peter the Great to stand in the middle of the city. The "Bronze Horseman" shows Peter on a rearing horse stomping on a snake. The reptile represents the backwardness that typified Russia when Peter took charge of the country. Peter's statue is so important to the city's residents that during the siege of World War II, they used lumber that was needed for fuel to protect the statue from German bombing.

St. Petersburg became a great center of intellectual and cultural life. For over two centuries, Russia's greatest composers, dancers, artists, novelists, poets, and scientists lived and worked in St. Petersburg. By the outbreak of World War II, the city was home to 60 institutions of higher learning, 103 technical schools, 25 theaters, 37 museums, 107 scientific research institutions, and the Kirov Ballet, the world's greatest ballet company.

Although St. Petersburg was an imperial city, the vast majority of its citizens lived in desperate poverty—slaves to the landowning minority. Many were people with no political or economic freedom. By the beginning of the 19th century, the peasants, the workers, and some members of the army were ready to join together to fight for a fairer share of Russia's riches. Their ambitions were stirred by the same revolutionary thinking that had fostered the revolutions in North America and France in the 1700s.

These ideas were especially important to the artists and writers of St. Petersburg. In the early 1800s the seeds of the Russian Revolution were sown. By the late 19th century the czar's revolutionary opponents were followers of a new political and economic philosophy. Calling themselves Bolsheviks or Communists, they fol-

lowed the writings of two men, Karl Marx and Friedrich Engels, who believed that the wealth of a nation should be controlled by all the people, not just a few. To Russians this meant that the czar must be overthrown and a new government, representing the entire population, be put into power.

A demonstration by Bolshevik supporters in St. Petersburg

19

Naval officers before the storming of the Winter Palace

In 1917, two Bolshevik leaders, Leon Trotsky and V. I. Lenin, mobilized their supporters and began a revolution against the czar. The Bolsheviks led uprisings throughout Russia. The soldiers, the workers, and the intellectuals of St. Petersburg played major roles in the Bolshevik Revolution. Their group also included the sailors aboard the battleship *Aurora*, which was anchored in the St. Petersburg harbor. In early March, the *Aurora* fired on the Winter Palace, and the Revolution was complete. On March 15, 1917, Czar Nicholas II abdicated his throne and the Communists installed their own government, with Lenin as its leader. The Russian Empire was renamed the Union of Soviet Socialist Republics—the Soviet Union.

For the first few years after the Revolution, it appeared that the personal freedoms the Bolsheviks had fought for—the right to vote, wider distribution of property, uncensored art and literature, a more prosperous life for industrial workers and peasant farmers—had been achieved. St. Petersburg experienced a cultural and economic rebirth after years of devastating poverty under the czars.

This newfound freedom was short-lived. Instead of building a government where all the people were represented, Lenin and his associates were as oppressive as the czars before them, ruthlessly suppressing anyone who opposed them. From that point on, power in Russia would reside with dictators as cruel and powerful as the leaders the Bolsheviks had worked so hard to overthrow.

In 1914, at the outbreak of World War I, the Russians had changed the name of St. Petersburg to Petrograd. They thought that St. Petersburg sounded too much like a city in Germany, the country they were at war against. The war that followed would bring many more changes to the city.

★ ★ ★

The new industry—the first tractor produced at the Stalingrad Tractor Works

3

THE SOONER RUSSIA IS CRUSHED, THE BETTER

During World War I (1914–1918), Finland, Latvia, Estonia, and Lithuania, with the help of Germany, split from the Russian Empire. After the war, the Baltic nations, as they were called, retained their independence, along with Poland and Bessarabia. The Finnish-Soviet border was now only 20 miles from Petrograd. Although the war was over, Russian bitterness toward Germany remained because of Germany's involvement in freeing the Baltic states.

Fearing a hostile neighbor so close to the capital, in 1918 Lenin ordered the capital of the Soviet Union moved to Moscow, the interior city on which Peter the Great had turned his back in 1703. In 1924 the name of Petrograd was officially changed to Leningrad to honor Lenin at the time of his death.

After Lenin's death, leadership of the Soviet Union passed to Joseph Stalin. Stalin imposed an iron will on the country. He made the Soviet Union a police state. Anyone who questioned his author-

Workers put together a newspaper against the background of a collective farm

ity was shot or imprisoned. The Communists' original goals for the Revolution had been the redistribution of land from the nobility to the peasants and the involvement of the workers in the management of industry. Joseph Stalin believed the only way to insure that these goals were met was to use force.

For young people living in the Soviet Union under the new

Young women at May Day rally carry rifles, a symbol of Stalin's belief in using force to meet his goals.

A car rolls off an assembly line at a plant in Gorki as part of Stalin's industrialization campaign.

government, life was very regimented. Proud of their national reputation in ballet, theater, and sports, the Communist party sought to train young people in these fields from an early age. All schools were run by the government. Children with special talents were identified in elementary school and ordered to attend high schools that would train them in specific fields.

Young people were also recruited for the Communist party. They were sent to special camps, indoctrinated to worship Stalin as a hero, and rewarded for turning over to authorities any information about adults who criticized Stalin and his administration— even their own parents.

Under the new regime, Leningrad's manufacturing grew tremendously. Most of the factories were devoted to heavy industry. At the largest of these, the Kirov Works, for example, thousands of workers lived in spartan conditions right at the plant. By 1940 the Soviet Union ranked third in the world in the production of steel, aluminum, and electricity, trailing only the United States and Germany. The nation was number one in rubber production and ranked second in oil and machine building.

Leningrad was the leading industrial city of the Soviet Union. However, almost nothing was produced in Leningrad's factories— or those of any other Russian city— to make life easier for Russian citizens. The factories of Leningrad were churning out materials for war, not peace.

As it had been for centuries, Germany was the enemy. The German Empire and the Russian Empire had long fought for control of the Baltic Sea. In the 20th century, the animosity between the two nations took on a new dimension. Under Hitler, who had come to power in the early 1930s, Germany had become a Fascist nation. Fascists believed in a strong dictator who used the military to control the political and economic life of a country. The Communists, on the other hand, believed that a country should be ruled by the proletariat, or common people. Hitler, as a Fascist, hated communism. Stalin, a Communist, hated fascism, or Nazism as it was called in Germany.

During most of the 1930s the two countries merely watched each other. Stalin was absorbed in his five-year plans, goading Russian workers, through force and fear, to even higher industrial quotas. Hitler was embarking on a campaign of territorial conquest abroad and the intimidation and eventually the mass murder of Jews within the German Reich.

Yet Stalin had not forgotten the hated Treaty of Brest-Litovsk, signed between Germany and Russia in 1917. He had not forgotten the loss of the Baltic states — Latvia, Lithuania, Estonia — and part of Poland. Nor was he happy to have the border with Finland, the traditional enemy of the Russians, so close to Leningrad. Stalin wanted to regain those lands. In 1939 he saw his chance. In a surprise move, he signed a nonaggression pact with Adolf Hitler.

Both men were buying time. Neither had truly changed nor forgotten his hatred of the other's country. Both had territorial goals. Stalin wanted control of the Baltic. Hitler wanted to conquer Poland and western Europe without Russian interference.

Shortly after signing the treaty, both men unleashed their armies on other nations. The factories of Leningrad worked overtime, grinding out guns and ammunition for "Winter War" between Russia and Finland. In a matter of months the Red Army had conquered 175,000 square miles (453,250 square kilometers) and added 20 million people to the Soviet Union. Latvia, Lithuania, and Estonia were recaptured, as were Finland's Karelian Isthmus and the mineral-rich region of Bessarabia.

Women at a munitions factory unload shell casings for use in the Winter War.

Soviet tanks patrol the streets of a village in the Ukraine as Hitler's army approaches.

Meanwhile, Hitler sent the powerful German army, the *Wehrmacht*, to attack Poland and a host of western European countries. His *blitzkrieg*—"lightning war"—meant swift conquest of Belgium, Norway, Denmark, the Netherlands, France, and several other nations in 1939 and 1940. As the Germans conquered even more land, many Soviet generals and diplomats became concerned that Hitler would break the treaty with Russia and attack the Soviet Union. If he were to do so, they all agreed that the focal point for his attack would be Leningrad. Not only was the border most vulnerable near the city, but Hitler "entertained an irrational hatred for Leningrad,"[1] perhaps because the city was the birthplace of communism, the archenemy of fascism.

Stalin refused to acknowledge any threat to the Soviet Union from Hitler, even though, by 1941, the Germans had possession of Bulgaria, Yugoslavia, and Romania. Germany's army was moving closer and closer to the Russian borders. To Stalin's generals it seemed inevitable that Russia would be next. To contradict the leader, however, meant at least losing one's job, and often resulted in exile or execution. The terror of Stalin's rule in the 1930s had demonstrated to Russian officers how impossible and even dangerous it was to disagree with the Russian dictator.

Yet the generals were correct. A close reading of Hitler's master plan, found in his book *Mein Kampf,* which was readily available, showed the Führer's plans for Russia. Adolf Hitler had written in 1924, Germany must expand, must have *lebensraum*—living space. As for where that space would come from, he wrote that "we are bound to think first of Russia and her border states."[2] As in much of his thinking, Hitler's hatred of the Soviet Union came from racial and religious prejudice. He called the Slavs a "mass of born slaves" and bolshevism a "Jewish plot."[3] The pact with Russia was never more than a temporary convenience for Hitler. As early as July 1940, he had told his generals that "the sooner Russia is crushed, the better," and assured them that if they would "just kick in the door, the whole rotten structure would collapse."[4]

In December 1940 Hitler began preparation for an attack on Russia. In an executive order dated December 18, he told his generals to "be prepared even before the conclusion of the war against England to crush Soviet Russia in a rapid campaign."[5] British spies operating in Germany found out about the plan and passed the news along to Winston Churchill, prime minister of England. Churchill warned Stalin of Hitler's plans to attack. At the same time, Stalin's own spies were reporting a major military buildup by the Germans along the borders of the Baltic states.

By the spring of 1941 it was clear to everyone but Stalin that Hitler would break the Soviet treaty and attack the Soviet Union. As Churchill later wrote, "Stalin and his commissars showed themselves the most completely outwitted bunglers of the Second World War."[6] Stalin continued to treat Germany as a friend. During the month of April the USSR sent Germany 208,000 tons of grain; 90,000 tons of oil; 8,300 tons of cotton; 6,340 tons of nickel, copper, and tin; and 4,000 tons of rubber,[7] all materials that Russia would need desperately when Germany invaded.

Of course, Hitler planned to attack Moscow because it was the enemy's capital city. But since Leningrad was closer to the border, Hitler planned that the city of czars and revolution would fall first.

In setting out to conquer the Soviet Union, Hitler wanted to do more than take over another country. Hitler's conquest of Russia was to be part of a Nazi crusade to wipe out communism. The Wehrmacht would not wage a strictly military battle and then allow life to go on under German military rule as had happened elsewhere. Hitler told his generals, "Communism is an enormous danger for our future. We must forget the concept of comradeship between soldiers. A Communist is no comrade before nor after battle. This is a war of extermination."[8] At the Nuremberg Trials held after World War II, it was revealed that Hitler had further ordered "that every Bolshevik commissar be executed without trial, and the Soviet intelligentsia wiped out in its entirety." As the Wehrmacht positioned itself to attack the Soviet Union, the SS, Hitler's special murder units, lined up behind it, prepared to kill all Jews and Communists captured by the army. Leningrad's citizenry contained many Jews. For these people especially, the city's battle against the Germans was from the beginning a fight for survival.

As one of the coldest springs in Russian history gave way finally to summer, Stalin still refused to act. The last snow fell in June, and at last Leningrad's annual "white nights" began. In the northernmost part of the city, June days are eighteen or nineteen hours long, and people emerging from the long, dark winter become giddy from the sun and warmth.

June 1941 was no exception, and the balmy days almost eased the tension caused by the rumors of war. However, for Kliment Y. Voroshilov, commander in chief of the Soviet military forces grouped around Leningrad, and Andrey Zhdanov, the Leningrad Communist party chief, the "white nights" brought increased vigilance. Both were convinced that the Germans would strike, and that the target would be their city.

Residents of Leningrad prepare for the coming Nazi invasion

4

THE ENEMY IS AT THE GATES OF LENINGRAD

At 3:30 A.M. on June 22, 1941, three million German soldiers attacked the Baltic border of the Soviet Union. It was the last of Hitler's blitzkrieg strikes and the most massive military attack in all of history. The Russians were caught in a state of total unpreparedness. As the greatest chronicler of the battle has written, "They had no prepared scheme on which to fall back in event of sudden Nazi attack because *Stalin had decreed that there would be no Nazi attack.* If a dictator decrees that there will be no attack, an officer who prepares for one is liable to execution as a traitor."[1]

The German troops moved across the border, meeting little resistance. Invading through the Baltic provinces was wise because

the Lithuanians, Latvians, and Estonians had little love for Russia and surrendered easily. Army Group Nord, the name for the German forces under the command of Field Marshal Wilhelm Ritter von Leeb, expected to capture Leningrad by July. Within the first

Residents of Odessa greet Red Army soldiers on their way to the front.

five days after the attack, the German army had penetrated deep into Soviet territory; half the Russian air force was destroyed. Von Leeb appeared to be nearing his goal.

Stalin, meanwhile, was scrambling to protect Moscow. Some

observers believed that he was ready to sacrifice Leningrad if necessary. Stalin, after all, shared Moscow's dislike of much of what Leningrad stood for—"all that was new, progressive and stylish."[2] He in turn represented for Leningrad all that was distasteful about Moscow—"the symbol of red tape, backwardness, crudeness, vulgarity and provinciality."[3] Hitler planned to take Moscow after the fall of Leningrad, but in spite of the immediate danger to the latter city, Stalin drained Leningrad of ammunition and supplies in order to fortify Moscow.

By early July, Andrey Zhdanov was working feverishly to prepare Leningrad to withstand the oncoming German assault. During the last days of June and the first days of July, hundreds of thousands of children were evacuated directly into the path of the oncoming German army; over half those who left had to be reevacuated into the city later that summer as the Germans circled closer. In addition, the Germans successfully bombed trainloads of fleeing children, killing 2,000 in one devastating raid on a train in Yedrovo.

Desperate to strengthen the fortifications around Leningrad as the German army advanced toward the city, Zhdanov decided to build a new line of defense, the Luga Line, along the Luga River, approximately 75 miles (121 kilometers) southwest of Leningrad. Zhdanov mobilized 30,000 citizens of Leningrad, mostly women and students, to build the 200-mile- (322-kilometer-) long defense. Other Leningraders prepared the city for attack, building enough air-raid shelters to hold nearly a million people and digging slit trenches to protect another 700,000.

Zhdanov called for volunteers to defend the Luga Line. By mid-July tens of thousands of men, women, and teenagers had joined a new regiment called the People's Volunteers. Short on training and guns, they were nevertheless energized by the knowl-

Red Army soldiers pass the bodies of dead soldiers as the war with Germany rages.

The women of Leningrad constructing barricades outside the city

edge that they alone stood between Leningrad and disaster. Colonel B. V. Bychevsky described his daughter, a freshman at Leningrad University, and her friends when they returned from the Luga Line. They had gone off to the task cheerful and optimistic, viewing it as something like a trip to a summer camp. They returned "weary to exhaustion, their clothes in rags, their bodies aching, their hands raw, their feet bruised, black with dirt, heavy with sweat."[4] Another girl, a high-school student, wrote of her work on the Luga Line this way: "We worked [in the summer] digging trenches. We were machine-gunned and some of us were killed, but we carried on, though we weren't used to this work."[5]

Other teenagers, particularly members of the Communist party's youth group, Komsomol, were enlisted as fire fighters and air-raid wardens as German shells fell on the city. A 17-year-old fire fighter later remembered summer nights on the roof of a building: "It was so quiet. Hardly any cars in the street. Strange. I felt as though I were flying over the city—a silver city, each roof and each spire engraved against the sky. And the blimps! On the ground they looked like sausages, fat and green. But at night, in the air, they swam like white whales under the clouds."[6]

The Germans reached the Luga Line in three weeks, but there they were halted. From the middle of July to the first week in August the Luga Line held. The People's Volunteers, at enormous cost in lives, held off the Wehrmacht. Writers, artists, poets, and children kept the Germans from their beloved city. Dmitry Shostakovich, the great Russian composer, tried unsuccessfully to volunteer. As he put it, "Up to now I have known only peaceful work; now I am ready to take up arms. Only by fighting can we save humanity from destruction."[7]

Hitler's plans for a July celebration of a Russian defeat had to

*Children
evacuated from
Leningrad
exercise in the
safety of their
country shelter.*

be shelved. But spirit and youth were ultimately no match for the German army. On August 8 von Leeb hurtled 29 German army divisions against the Soviets in a major attack. The Luga Line fell. On August 21 the Germans reached Chudovo, cutting off the main rail line between Moscow and Leningrad. On August 30 the Germans reached the Neva River and captured the rail station at Mga, effec-

tively cutting Leningrad off from the rest of the USSR. When Shlis-selburg on the shore of Lake Ladoga fell to the Germans on September 3, 1941, the entrapment of Leningrad was complete. Except for dangerous flights or uncertain water passage over Lake Ladoga, both under German fire, there was no way to exit from or enter the city. The siege had begun.

The people of Leningrad relied on trains to bring them food and supplies.

Stunned by the news from the Leningrad front, Stalin ordered that the city be mined. All major military posts, naval stations, ships, and ammunition factories were prepared to be blown up. If Leningrad could not be saved, at least the Germans would find nothing useful. Stalin also replaced Voroshilov with Marshal Georgy Zhukov. Zhukov was determined never to surrender the city. Nevertheless, on September 4 Stalin notified Churchill that "the enemy is at the gates of Leningrad."[8]

Although efforts had been made to evacuate children and the elderly, the movement had not been highly successful. Furthermore, refugees had flooded into the city from the surrounding countryside, driven there by the German onslaught. By the time the city was cut off, its population stood close to three million, just as it had in June. Leningrad had no food supplies, and the Russian winter was rapidly approaching. Under the circumstances, Hitler made a calculated decision—to starve the city into submission. As one of his generals recorded in his diary, "It is the Führer's firm decision to level Leningrad and Moscow and make them uninhabitable so as to relieve us of the necessity of feeding the populations through the winter."[9] Starvation, he reasoned, would mean fewer military losses for the Germans. Shelling of the city would continue, both to frighten and kill the inhabitants, but the large panzer divisions necessary for an invasion were sent toward Moscow by the middle of September.

The Russian defense of Leningrad was only a part of the war effort in Europe. Since 1939 Great Britain, France, Belgium, Denmark, the Netherlands, Poland, and a host of allies had fought desperately against Germany. One by one the Germans had defeated all but Great Britain. In December 1941, with the bombing of Pearl Harbor, the United States entered the war. From the beginning of

*Firemen work
to control a blaze
started by Nazi
bombs.*

БОМБОУБЕЖИЩЕ

Children are entertained with a story while taking shelter during a bomb raid.

the American entry, President Franklin D. Roosevelt worked closely with British prime minister Winston Churchill to develop the most efficient strategy for defeating the Germans. Most of their plans involved attacks on the German army in western Europe and depended upon the Russian army to maintain pressure on Germany from the east.

The Russians fought hard along their battlefront. To many war historians the pivotal battle of the European war occurred during the winter of 1942–1943, when the Soviets maintained the defense of Stalingrad, eventually saving that city and killing a half-million German troops. During 1941 this Soviet victory was still far in the future. As World War II raged throughout Europe, the Germans settled down to wait for Leningrad to starve.

A man in Leningrad with his precious daily ration of bread.

5

LENINGRAD IS DYING

On July 18, 1941, less than a month after the German attack, the Soviet government ordered food rationing in all major cities. With food supplies endangered by the German advance, it was a prudent move. Unfortunately, in those summer months, the party leaders in Leningrad did not anticipate how critical the food shortage in the city would become. The rationing was not strict enough. No attempt was made to insure even distribution of the city's remaining supplies. In the early days of the German blitzkrieg, stores were emptied by those with the money to do so. All summer, Leningrad's restaurants served sumptuous meals of meats, with little worry about the fact that the city's supplies were rapidly running out.

When the city was cut off from the rest of the nation in August, an inventory of the remaining food showed that there was enough flour for 17 days, cereals (millet, rice, semolina, buckwheat)

Too sick to walk, a woman is dragged through the streets of Leningrad on a sled by a friend.

for 29 days, fish for 16 days, meat for 25 days, and butter for 28 days. Faced with these grim statistics, the authorities cut the rations on September 2. Factory workers were allotted 21 ounces (594 grams) of bread per day, office workers 14 ounces (396 grams), children and dependents 10½ ounces (297 grams). Each slice of bread weighed approximately 3 ounces (85 grams). In addition, each person was allotted 3 pounds (1.4 kilograms) of meat and cereal per month, 1½ pounds (679 grams) of fats, and 5 ounces (142 grams) of candy or sugar. Twenty-one ounces (594 grams) of bread provided only 1,000 calories; an adult worker needed a minimum of 3,000 calories per day.

All of the countries at war rationed food. However, no other area inside or outside Russia verged on starvation. In England, for example, people were restricted to ¾ of a pound (340 grams) of beef or 8 ounces (226.4 grams) of lamb chops per week, but plenty of fish and cheaper meat, such as liver, were available. Germans were rationed to one pound of meat per person per week, but there was no shortage of bread. In the United States, the strictest rationing applied to sugar, butter, and meat. On average, Americans consumed 140 pounds of meat per person annually during the war, far less than had been their habit in the prewar years, but far more than their Russian allies. Furthermore, Americans never suffered from lack of food, only from lack of choice. Because of victory gardens—backyard gardens encouraged by the government—there were always enough vegetables to go around.

On September 8, disaster struck Leningrad again. German bombers hit the Badayev warehouses, where most of the city's reserves of food were kept. All of the city's 2,500 tons of sugar melted in the fire caused by the bombs. (In the winter, when people were truly starving, they dug up the "Badayev earth" and ate it, hoping to get some nutrition from the melted sugar.) Overnight the critical situation became desperate. Nearly 3.4 million people—civilians and soldiers—were in danger of starving to death. On September 10, to deal with the situation, Moscow sent Dmitri V. Pavlov to Leningrad, placing him in charge of food supplies. Pavlov immediately cut rations again on September 12—to 17½ ounces (495 grams) of bread per day for workers and proportionately lower amounts for others. This amount of bread provided fewer than one-third of the calories needed for an adult worker. (There would be three more rationing reductions that fall—on October 1, November 13, and November 20, when workers' bread rations were cut to 9 ounces [255 grams], with others receiving only half that.) By cutting rations to this level, Pavlov insured that the food supplies would last longer—but at these levels, people would eventually starve to death.

To help get the situation under control, Pavlov ordered a complete inventory of all food left in the city. Every nook and cranny of every storehouse was searched. Simply by sweeping the floors of empty grain elevators, Pavlov regained 500 tons of grain. He declared that anything "digestible and with calories" would be considered food.[1] He also ordered new ration cards for every citizen, believing—probably correctly—that panic about the city's situation had led to forged cards. He made any further forgeries a capital offense, that is, punishable by death. One woman who worked in a government printing shop was found with 100 ration cards. She was quickly taken out and shot.

No one could buy any food without a ration card, and to keep track of the city's population, new ration cards were issued each month. A common trick for obtaining a second ration card was to report that a card had been lost or stolen. In October there were

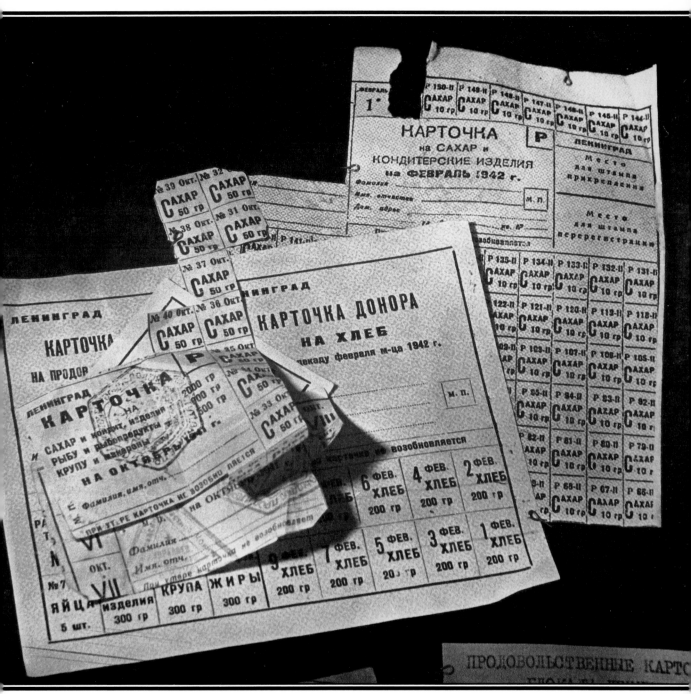

A ration card used during the siege

Soldiers look over a shipment of dried fruit sent to the vitamin-starved people of Leningrad.

5,000 such reported losses; in November, 13,000; and in December, 24,000. To put an end to this fraud, Pavlov decreed that no lost or stolen ration cards would be replaced. For those people who had truly lost their cards, this rule meant almost certain death after December. A person's ration card became his or her most precious possession. In addition, each person had to register with a specific bakery at which to receive his or her ration. This insured that food would be distributed evenly throughout the city.

Although the amount of the bread ration in September seemed adequate, the composition of the bread made it far from nutritious. Pavlov ordered the following recipe in mid-September: 52% rye flour, 30% oats, 8% barley, 5% soya, 5% malt. Normal, good-tasting, nutritious bread contained wheat, yeast, and some form of sweetener—sugar, molasses, or honey. Bread of the type that Pavlov prescribed was heavy, difficult to digest, and lacking in nutrients. The malt had been intended for breweries; with the breweries closed, Pavlov used it as a substitute for flour. By the end of October, Pavlov's recipe was even worse: 67% rye flour, 8% oats, 4% soya, 12% malt, 4% flax cake, and 5% moldy grain (grain that had been dredged from sunken transports along the bottom of the Neva River and Lake Ladoga). Even Pavlov admitted that the bread "reeked of mold and malt."[2] Confided one Leningrader to his diary, "We are eating bread as heavy as cobble-stones and bitter with cottonseed-oil cake."[3]

Teenagers were the worst off because they received the same ration as toddlers and preteens, even though their bodies required far more. One mother, Yelena Skryabina, confided to her diary her fears for the life of her 16-year-old son, who had lost all energy and will to live as he slowly starved to death on a ration of 7 ounces (199 grams) of bread per day.

As the bread ration dwindled, people would do, sell, or barter anything to get more. Eating became so important that rituals grew up around each mouthful of food. One citizen described the various ways Leningraders approached their rations: "Bread can be eaten in different ways. One can eat it by biting off a piece or by breaking off crumbs. Others cut it: some into thin transparent slices, some into thick squares. . . . The thoughtless ones eat the bread before they have even left the bakery, the others—they are in the minority—divide the ration into 3 parts: for breakfast, lunch and dinner. To know that one can eat one's own piece of bread right away, and stop oneself from doing it, is an act of heroism."[4]

Animals suffered almost immediately. Crows, pigeons, cats, and dogs virtually disappeared from the city. They either starved or were eaten. The poet Vera Inber wrote in her diary about encountering a friend who told her that his daughter had spent the whole evening in a cellar looking for a cat—not to be a pet, but to be the family's meal.[5] Horses fared no better. Many were slaughtered and eaten. Others, needed for transportation, were reduced to the same kind of starvation rations as their masters. Some were fed bundles of twigs boiled in hot water and covered with salt. Others were fed cakes of peat shavings and flour dust.

By October no living being in Leningrad had enough to eat. Even high party officials and army officers, typically the last to suffer, were hungry. They ate military rations: a pound of bread per day plus a bowl of soup, some cereal, and occasionally sugar in their tea. Pavlov desperately looked for food substitutes. Cottonseed cake that was to be used as ships' fuel had the poison burned out of it and became first 3% of the bread recipe and eventually 10%. Bulbs from the city's botanical gardens, stinging nettles, and cattle feed were all ground into human food. When 2,000 tons of sheep guts

After their school is hit by a bomb, schoolchildren take their classroom outside.

were found in a warehouse, they were converted to meat jelly; it was vile and smelled, but people still ate it.

The citizens of Leningrad invented their own foods. In recounting the worst days of the siege, Pavlov wrote that people "would go through medicine chests in search of castor oil, hair oil, vaseline or glycerine; they would make soup or jelly out of carpenter's glue (scraped off wallpaper or broken-up furniture)."[6] By the end of the fall, no woman in Leningrad wore lipstick; it had all been eaten. Coffee grounds were made into pancakes. Belts and shoes and bookcovers, anything leather, were eaten in the form of meat jelly. A visitor to the home of Yuri Panaleyev spotted his briefcase and asked if she could take it. The next day he received from her a small dish of meat jelly—and the metal clasp, as proof that this, too, had not gone into the food.

As October wore on, the hunger grew more acute, and deaths from starvation began to mount. Nikolai Chukovsky described the slow death by starvation:

> The first day or two or three were the worst.... If a man had nothing but a slice of bread to eat, he suffered terrible hunger pangs the first day. And the second. But gradually the pain faded into quiet despondency, a gloom that had no ending, a weakness that advanced with frightening rapidity. What you did yesterday you could not do today. You found yourself surrounded by obstacles too difficult to overcome. The stairs were too steep to climb.... Each day the weakness grew. But awareness did not decline. You saw yourself from a distance. You knew what was happening, but you could not halt it. You saw your body changing, the legs wasting to toothpicks, the arms vanishing, the breasts turning into empty bags. Skirts slipped from the hips. Trousers would not stay up. Strange bones appeared. Or the opposite—you puffed up. You could no longer wear your shoes. Your neighbor had to help you to your feet. Your cheeks looked as though

Washing clothes in melted ice water during the siege

they were bursting. Your neck was too thick for your collar. But it was nothing except wind and water. There was no strength in you. Some said it came from drinking too much. Half of Leningrad was wasting away, the other half was swelling from the water drunk to fill empty stomachs.[7]

Children working in a munitions plant were a common sight during the war years in Russia.

The official name for starvation at the Leningrad hospitals was "alimentary dystrophy." Hospitals rapidly filled to overflowing, although doctors, weakened like everyone else, could do little to help the suffering. Most people died at home, at work, in the breadlines, their bodies simply giving out. Eleven thousand people died in November; in December the death toll was 53,000, more people than had died in the city in all of 1940. As the poet Olga Bergolts wrote in her diary: "Death. Death. Everywhere death. In Leningrad only one thing is happening—dying. Leningrad is dying. Slowly and painfully, the city is perishing."[8]

As the death toll mounted, mass graves were dynamited to hold the bodies. In many cases, however, surviving family members did not have the strength to transport their dead to the cemeteries. There was no fuel for cars or streetcars. As Bergolts described it, "From Moscow Station lined all the way up to the Alexander Nevsky Monastery, were buses, frozen and buried under snow, like corpses. It was impossible to imagine that there had been a time when they had moved."[9] Those who could dragged the bodies of loved ones to the cemeteries on sleds. Wood was needed for fuel, not coffins, so bodies were wrapped in blankets or old clothes. Vera Inber described a visit to the cemetery: "The bodies are wrapped in sheets, in blankets, in tablecloths, sometimes even curtains. Once I saw a small bundle wrapped in paper and tied with a string. It was very small, the body of a child."[10] Nearly all the corpses were barefoot; according to Bergolts, "Only those alive and walking the paths of a dead, freezing, unyielding city needed overshoes."[11]

There was another incentive for failing to bury bodies in the city cemeteries. As long as the authorities did not know that the person had died, relatives were free to use his or her ration card. A youngster told a neighbor that "Papa and Mama died, and we and

Grandmother hid their bodies in the attic and now we have five ration cards for three persons."[12] That such deceit was punishable by death was unimportant to a starving, grief-stricken child.

On the whole, young children fared no worse than, if not better than, adults, probably because parents were willing to sacrifice to the point of starving to death themselves in order to give their children extra food. The reverse was also true. An inspector at a boarding school found that the students, weak as they were, often took half their ration and walked home with it after classes in order to share with family members.

By January 1942, the official estimate was that 3,000 to 4,000 people daily were dying of starvation. In reality, the death toll may have been as high as 10,000 a day. The birthrate in Leningrad declined sharply. In 1942, births dropped by one-third; they dropped another quarter in 1943.

There was surprisingly little crime during the first few months of the siege. As the hunger grew worse, however, there were isolated reports of people murdered for bread or ration cards. To keep the city's morale as high as possible, and to prevent panic, most stories of crime and cowardice were not published. After the war, all accounts of the siege were doctored by the Communist party to present a picture of perfect Communist efficiency and control in dealing with the crisis.

In truth, however, a black market flourished in a darker quarter of the city, the Haymarket. Food could be bought there for exorbitant prices. For 100 rubles (16 dollars), for example, a glass of melted sugar and dirt—Badayev earth—could be purchased. More sinister was the meat sold in the Haymarket. Corpses in the mass graves often lacked limbs; it was believed that this human flesh went into the meat patties sold at the Haymarket. Where else could the

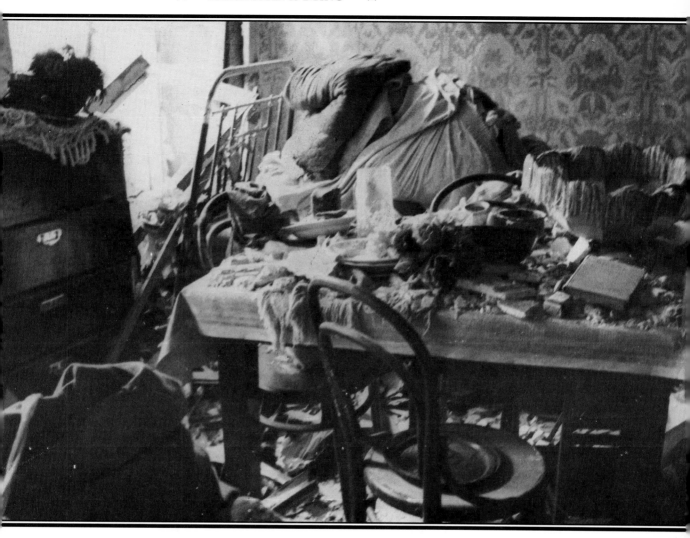

meat have come from?

Rumors of cannibalism spread through the city, and parents kept a close eye on their children, forbidding them to go out alone. Occasionally, people told stories of parents who, crazed with hunger, killed and ate their children. No one was sure these stories were true, but as the hunger grew worse, anyone could believe

A bombed apartment displays the damage caused by German shelling

them. And then there were sights like the severed head of a small girl lying on a snow pile outside a cemetery. It was easy to believe that her body had been stolen for food. Soldiers, who received the highest rations, were supposed targets of cannibal traders because they were healthier. Wrote the poet Daniel Andreyev,

*A street scene
after a Nazi
bombing mission*

We have known everything...
That in the Russian language there is
No word for that mad war winter...
And we learned, too, about cannibalism.[13]

A train hauls food and supplies over tracks once used for streetcars.

6

THE ROAD OF LIFE

To starving Leningraders, hunger was intensified by numbing cold as fall gave way to winter. The winter of 1941–1942 proved to be one of the coldest in Russian history. For several days in October the temperature dropped below zero. Ski Day, a city holiday each year celebrating the first snowfall to reach four inches, occurred on October 31, the earliest ever. Fuel was as impossible to obtain as food. The authorities ordered that the temperature in apartments be set no higher than 54°F (12°C), in offices at 50°F (10°C), and in factories at 47°F (8.3°C). They needn't have bothered. In reality, the temperatures were much lower.

Water pipes burst, and by November all water had to be carried by hand from holes cut in the ice of the Neva River and its tributaries. (In many families this job was given to children.) Nor was there any electricity. The days were short anyway, and in the cold fall and winter, everything seemed gray because there were no lights. In the evening, as the official history of the city records, "the city sank into impenetrable darkness."[1] People lived in one room, huddled around *burzhuikas*, small potbellied stoves. They burned books, furniture, fences—anything to stay warm. Most people wore their overcoats night and day, indoors and out. A surgeon at Leningrad hospital "frequently had to do blood transfusions in a fur coat and a fur hat and keep [his] hands warm by putting them in warm water."[2]

The effects of the terrible cold were almost as devastating as the effects of hunger. A university student described the feeling of being cold: "One gets up with it, one walks with it, one goes to bed with it. It seems to wander around somewhere under the skin; it penetrates the bones and sometimes it seems as if it even enters the brain."[3] In spite of the hunger and cold, some aspects of ordinary life went on. One of these was school.

In an essay about her daily life at the Tambov Street School, a pupil graphically detailed the effects of the cold:

Our classes continued on the "Round the Stove" principle. If you wanted a seat near the stove or under the stovepipe, you had to come early. The place facing the stove door was reserved for the teacher. You sat down and were suddenly seized by a wonderful feeling of well-being; the warmth penetrated through your skin, right into your bones. It was agony to get up and go to the blackboard. At the blackboard it was so cold and dark, and your hand, imprisoned in its heavy glove, went all numb and rigid and refused to obey. The chalk kept falling out of your hand, and the lines were all crooked.[4]

Throughout the fall, Dmitri Pavlov and Andrey Zhdanov knew that only two things could help the people of Leningrad survive. Either the population had to be evacuated, or more supplies

To escape the freezing cold of winter, many people gathered around stoves and boilers to keep warm.

had to be brought in. When the Germans cut the rail lines connecting Leningrad to the rest of the Soviet Union, the city's leaders tried to develop an alternate route across Lake Ladoga. In Septem-

Wooden houses damaged by bombs are torn apart so the wood can be used for fuel.

ber they built a port at Osinovets on the western shore of the lake. Although the lake freighters had not previously hauled the majority of the city's supplies, they tried now to do the job. Under heavy enemy fire, the sailors and dockworkers of Lake Ladoga managed to transport 25,000 tons of food and fuel to Leningrad between September and November of 1941. Although it was not nearly enough, without it the city would surely have surrendered. Critical to the success of this operation was the train track running from Tikhvin to Novaya Ladoga, where the supplies were loaded onto ships.

On November 9, Tikhvin fell to the Germans. On November 15, ice on the lake made ship travel impossible. The end seemed at hand. With only a few day's food left, rations were cut one final time to their lowest point—an amount so small that it would not support life, only postpone death.

In the face of the crisis, Leningrad officials determined to use the Russian winter as their ally; the ice would save Leningrad. A road could be constructed across the lake from Osinovets in the west to Novaya Ladoga in the east. From there a road could be built east of the German forces at Tikhvin along an old forest track from Novaya Ladoga to Zaborye, the railhead for trains from Moscow. From the beginning the plan seemed to be a fantasy; the road, over 200 miles (322 kilometers) long, would have to be constructed in the middle of winter "through uninhabited bogs and occasional tiny villages."[5] From Novaya Ladoga, the food would go by convoy to Osinovets; from there it would travel over an antiquated suburban railroad to the city. This last leg would be nearly as hazardous as any other part of the trip. The prerevolutionary rail line would have to be fueled by hand. Trees would have to be cut on the spot to keep it going; the unseasoned fuel would not be effective.

Undaunted, Zhdanov ordered that work on the forest road begin at once. Meanwhile, the ice was carefully measured. With the temperature at 5°F (-15°C) for 24 hours, 4 inches (10 centimeters) of ice could form. To support a truck convoy, 12 inches (30 centimeters) of ice was needed, a thickness that would take eight days to form at subzero temperatures.

On November 19, with the ice only four inches thick, Captain Mikhail Nurov led soldiers in life jackets onto the ice, accompanied by horses and sleighs. Slowly they made their way to Kobona, where food supplies had been held since the lake became impassable. On November 20, they returned. The "Road of Life,"

Workers build rail lines to the bays and inlets around Leningrad so that supplies can be delivered by ship.

officially Military Highway 101, was open. Over a thousand horses and sleds made the trip in the first few days, each horse being able to draw 200 to 250 pounds (91 to 114 kilograms).

As heartwarming as it was to see new food coming into the city, it was not enough. Prior to the siege, Leningrad had consumed 2,000 tons of flour per day. The starvation level was 500 tons. The horses were bringing in a mere 100 tons.

On November 22, motorized vehicles were ordered onto the ice. Sixty trucks left Osinovets that day. Those that returned the next day carried nearly 30 tons of flour. In the first week of truck supplies, 800 tons of flour were brought into the city. In spite of the cold, many drivers drove with their doors open so that they could jump clear if their trucks broke through the ice. Forty trucks sank. In addition to the perils of ice travel, the suppliers had great difficulty on "the abominable forest road."[6] At some points, two trucks could not pass. When a truck became stuck in the heavy snow, the road was blocked for days.

And then, on December 9, the Red Army recaptured Tikhvin. Dmitri Pavlov later wrote, "Without exaggeration the defeat of the German fascist troops at Tikhvin saved from starvation thousands of people."[7] The rail line to Moscow was now open. Special trains marked "97," meaning they were taking food to Leningrad, sped north to relieve the city. New trucks weighing three tons were pressed into lake service. These trucks could travel up to 40 m.p.h. (64 k.p.h.) on the ice and make two to three trips a day. At the height of its success, the "Road of Life" carried 400 three-ton trucks a day.

On Christmas Eve 1941, Pavlov ordered a slight increase in the ration. It would be raised again on January 24, and again in February. The effects of starvation, however, did not end with the opening of the "Road of Life." For thousands of people, weakened by hunger in the fall and early winter, relief came too late. The death toll continued to mount as dysentery, pneumonia, and other diseases attacked wasted bodies. In January 1942, 166 members of the Leningrad city police died of starvation; in February over 200 died. A weekly report on the city's famous orchestra read, "The first violin is dying, the drummer died on the way to work, the French horn is near death."[8] Anna Vasileyva, a 15-year-old worker at the Kirov Factory, recalled that by January there was no work, and yet 3,000 workers stayed on at the plant, living in a stupor of hunger and cold. She remembered that "the first thing you would do [each

*The ice road on
Lake Ladoga*

morning] was to look around to see if everyone was there, if your friends were still alive. . . . Then you'd notice someone sitting in the chair beside the stove. At first he would look all right. Then you'd look closer and see that he was sitting there dead."[9]

Nor were the Leningraders free from shelling. Nearly every day German guns bombarded the city. Many civilians, in spite of their weakened condition, remained on active duty defending the

city's borders. Those who worked in the munitions factories were the most frequent targets. And thousands of Leningraders remained on active duty with the army just outside the city's gates.

On January 18 the ice road exceeded its quota for the first time, but the population of the city had shrunk to 2.2 million. On January 22 the official decision was made to evacuate 500,000 people over the ice road. Evacuation had the double benefit of getting

A supply point on the transport road to Leningrad

people to safety and reducing the population that would need to be fed. Only soldiers, essential factory workers, and government officials were to remain.

A Soviet mortar crew returns German fire

Evacuees were not permitted to leave on foot. As in everything else, the city's Communist officials wanted to keep track of the process. Children and old people were issued the first passes for the evacuation transports. Many who made it to the trains got no farther. Dead bodies were thrown out along the way. Nevertheless, hundreds of thousands of people were evacuated by April 12, the day the thawing ice made it dangerous to continue the evacuations. By the end of April, only 1.1 million people remained in the city.

When the ice melted, ships took over the trucks' work. Between May and November 1942, the Ladoga shipping lines carried over 700,000 tons of food, horses, and fuel to the city. By May, Leningraders had rations of meat, herring, sugar, and milk. Knowing that the war was far from over—the Red Army suffered serious losses at Sevastopol and in the Crimea in 1942, and the great victory at Stalingrad was still to come—the city worked feverishly to prepare for another winter. Posters listing edible plants hung on street corners, and children planted cabbage gardens on every available inch of land.

Leningrad continued to suffer heavy casualties from German shelling. For no matter how much the Germans had counted on starvation to conquer Leningrad, they had never ceased their artillery attacks on the city. The attack had been continuous, and as supply lines to the city reopened, the Germans intensified their shelling. Signs were posted that warned: "Citizens: In case of shelling, this side of the street is most dangerous." Yet, as time would tell, the Leningraders' stamina and will to survive would lead them out of danger.

The statue of Peter the Great emerges from the hill of sand built to protect it from German bombing.

7

LENINGRAD WILL ALWAYS STAND

As the second year of the siege began, the one million people left in Leningrad were far better prepared to withstand another winter of German blockade and bombardment. All but the most essential workers and soldiers had been evacuated. Food and fuel supplies had been built up over the summer to such an extent that for the rest of the war, Leningraders were actually better fed than their fellow citizens elsewhere in the Soviet Union.

Over the spring and summer of 1942, German offensives against Russian forces in the southern areas of the country had been successful. Although the Germans had come within a mile and a half of the center of downtown Leningrad, they were still unable to capture the city. Then, on November 18, just before deep winter set

81

in, Russian forces recaptured Shlisselburg, reestablishing direct rail connections with Moscow and the interior. Trains traveling on this line were subjected to heavy German fire because the German line had been pushed back to only 500 yards (450 meters) from the track. But the trains made it through, aided by an "elite military rail unit," Special Engine Column 48.[1]

In January 1943 the Red Army scored another major victory, this time at Stalingrad. On May Day, the annual Communist party holiday, the people of Leningrad celebrated their first official holiday since June 22, 1941. Their celebration was a bit premature. The Wehrmacht was not finished with the city. During July and August, Leningrad was subjected to the worst shelling yet. In spite of the danger, the people of Leningrad carried on. Fifteen-year-old Tamara Turanova, who worked in a munitions factory, described the shelling: "When a shell whistles, it means it's high up; it's only when it begins to sizzle, that you know there's going to be trouble."[2]

Still the Germans failed to conquer the city. And then the Red Army launched a counteroffensive. Named *Iskra,* "spark," after Lenin's revolutionary newspaper, this final assault by the Russians against the Wehrmacht was successful. On January 27, 1944, red, white, and blue rockets soared over Leningrad. After nearly 900 days, the "greatest siege in modern times, perhaps in all history"[3] was over. At the height of the siege, the composer Dmitry Shostakovich had broadcast an inspirational message to the people of Leningrad. He had said, "A feeling of deep conviction grows within me that Leningrad will always stand, that it will always be the bastion of my country."[4] Shostakovich's words proved to be prophetic.

★ ★ ★

Although Soviet historians have downplayed the number of people

The Red Army routs the Germans

who died of starvation during the worst days of the siege, some people estimate that a million people died from starvation alone, with perhaps another 750,000 dying from the bombs and shelling. In all of World War II, the combined British and American losses

Triumphant Red Army soldiers hoist a Soviet flag over a building in Schlisselburg after recapturing it from German forces.

totaled 800,000. There has never been another siege in history as devastating as that of Leningrad.

Thousands of Leningrad's war dead lie in the Piskarevsky Cemetery under an eternal flame and the words of Olga Bergolts:

Russian children taken hostage by the Germans are discovered by advancing Red Army troops.

85

Here lie the people of Leningrad,
Here are the citizens—men, women and children—
And beside them the soldiers of the Red Army
Who gave their lives
Defending you, Leningrad,
Cradle of Revolution.
We cannot number the noble
Ones who lie beneath the eternal granite,
But of those honored by this stone
Let no one forget, let nothing be forgotten.

Having demonstrated their bravery and loyalty during the siege, the citizens of Leningrad hoped that peacetime might bring relief from the grim dictatorship that Stalin had imposed upon them during the prewar years. In this they were sadly mistaken. As the primary historian of the siege has written, "Leningrad had survived the Nazis. Whether it could survive the Kremlin was not so clear."[5] Immediately after the defeat of Germany in 1945, Stalin ordered thousands of workers to return to Leningrad and established high production quotas for the shattered industrial plants of the city. Censorship and repression were as unyielding as ever.

To Leningraders, perhaps the most distressing aspect of the renewed censorship was the ban on poetry, artwork, and novels written about and during the siege. Stalin believed that tales of the horrors undergone in the city would reflect badly on the Communist party's preparation for the war. His animosity toward Leningrad had not disappeared during the war, but had only been sidetracked while he focused on Russia's military plight. He was well aware that few pictures of him hung in the city and that, throughout the crisis, the people of Leningrad had fought for their city, not for the glory of Stalin and his brand of Communism. By April 1944, the city's

*The Blue Hall in
the palace of
Catherine the
Great damaged
by German
vandals*

After the war, people wander through the scarred landscape of their beautiful city.

leaders had produced a museum exhibit commemorating Leningrad's experiences in the war; Stalin ordered that it be dismantled.

By 1944 the population of Leningrad had shrunk to less than a third of its prewar number. With the end of the war in sight, Stalin ordered that the population of the city be built up again. Using the same kind of five-year plan that he had enforced for industrial and agricultural production, he decreed that the city should grow to one million by the end of the year. He wanted the people to work in the industrial plants that he planned to rebuild.

Leningrad had been badly shelled by the Germans for nearly three years. From August 1941 to January 1944, as many as 2,500 shells a day had rained down on the city. Over 3,000 buildings had been destroyed. The city did not have enough intact housing to handle the influx of industrial workers, but Stalin did not care. He ordered money set aside to repair the historic palaces and imperial government buildings—the Hermitage and the Winter Palace, for example—to be used instead of building inexpensive modern apartment houses.

In 1946 the mayor of Leningrad and the city's party chief presented the central government in Moscow with a plan for the "renaissance" of Leningrad. The plan was ignored, but the rebuilding of the factories and the construction of yet additional substandard suburban housing continued as Stalin put even more demands on the city's factories. A reporter from *Newsweek* magazine, visiting the city in 1947, was told by his official Communist guide, "War destruction? Oh, that's all repaired."[6] Most of the grand palaces still stood, and the skyline remained the same, but the restoration that many citizens of Leningrad had hoped for did not take place.

Stalin's rule came to an end with his death in 1953. His successor, Nikita Khrushchev, allowed some commemoration of the siege. The museum exhibit was reopened in 1957, although many parts of it had been lost. The signs warning of shelling were posted again; to Leningraders, they were proud reminders of their bravery under fire.

Throughout the Cold War years, Leningrad went on much as before. By Communist order it was a city devoted to heavy industry, particularly defense manufacturing. At heart, however, it was a city proud of its heritage, with an unshakable identity forged in the grimmest days of the war. And once again Leningrad was a cultural mecca—the symphony, the Kirov Ballet, the Hermitage Museum, and the universities drew artists and scholars from across the Soviet Union and the world.

A popular joke in the city in the 1970s went like this: "Where were you born? St. Petersburg. Where were you educated? Petrograd. Where do you now live? Leningrad. Where do you want to live? St. Petersburg."[7] In 1991 the citizens of Leningrad got their wish: The city officially became St. Petersburg. And, as civil and political freedom grows throughout the Soviet Union, the complete history of the siege may at last come to light.

A momument to the children of Leningrad who died during the siege

SOURCE NOTES

✳ ✳ ✳

CHAPTER ONE

1. Harrison S. Salisbury, *The 900 Days: The Siege of Leningrad* (New York: Harper & Row, 1969), 490.
2. Ibid., 490.
3. Ibid.
4. Robert Leckie, *Delivered from Evil: The Saga of World War II* (New York: Harper & Row, 1987), 591-592.
5. Salisbury, 391.

CHAPTER TWO

1. Robert K. Massie, *Peter the Great: His Life and World* (New York: Ballantine Books, 1980), 602.
2. Ibid., 365.
3. Howard LaFay and Dick Durrance, "Russia's Window On The West: Leningrad," *The National Geographic Magazine* (May 1971), 639.

CHAPTER THREE

1. William K. Klingaman, *1941: Our Lives in a World on the Edge* (New York: Harper & Row, 1988), 305.
2. Nicholas Bethell, *Russia Besieged* (Alexandria, Va.: Time-Life Books, 1980), 21.
3. Ibid., 22.
4. Ibid., 23.
5. Klingaman, 19.
6. Ibid., 235.
7. Salisbury, 63.
8. Klingaman, 236.

CHAPTER FOUR

1. Salisbury, 78.
2. Ibid., 126.
3. Ibid.
4. Ibid., 173.
5. Alexander Werth, *Russia at War: 1941–1945* (New York: E. P. Dutton, 1964), 352.
6. Salisbury, 168.
7. Leckie, 283.
8. Bethell, 23.
9. Ibid., 106.

1. Bethell, 110.
2. Salisbury, 370.
3. Leckie, 590.
4. Bethell, 120.
5. Salisbury, 390.
6. Werth, 136-137.
7. Salisbury, 376.
8. Bethell, 111.
9. Olga Bergolts, "A Walk Along the Neva: The Siege of Leningrad," *The Atlantic* (June 1960), 52.
10. Klingaman, 386.
11. Bergolts, 52.
12. Bethell, 116.
13. Salisbury, 481.

CHAPTER FIVE

1. Salisbury, 422.
2. "The Surgeons of Leningrad," *Time* (April 5, 1943), 46.
3. Bethell, 112.
4. Werth, 352.
5. Bethell, 112.
6. Salisbury, 413.
7. Ibid.
8. Ibid., 462.
9. Ibid., 489-490.

CHAPTER SIX

1. Salisbury, 554.
2. Werth, 136-137.
3. Leckie, 664.
4. Klingaman, 385.
5. Salisbury, 578.
6. "Russia: Three More Years," *Newsweek* (May 19, 1947), 38.
7. Bart McDowell, *Journey Across Russia: The Soviet Union Today* (Washington, D.C., National Geographic Society, 1977), 66.

CHAPTER SEVEN

FURTHER READING

⋆ ⋆ ⋆

Bethell, Nicholas. *Russia Besieged*. Alexandria, Va.: Time-Life Books, 1980.

Erickson, John. *The Road to Stalingrad: Stalin's War with Germany*. Boulder: Westview Press, 1984.

Gunther, John. *Inside Russia Today*. New York: Harper and Brothers, 1957.

Klingaman, William K. *1941: Our Lives in a World on the Edge*. New York: Harper & Row, 1988.

Leckie, Robert. *Delivered from Evil: The Saga of World War II*. New York: Harper & Row, 1987.

Massie, Robert K. *Peter the Great: His Life and World*. New York: Ballantine Books, 1980.

McDowell, Bart. *Journey Across Russia: The Soviet Union Today*. Washington, D.C.: National Geographic Society, 1977.

Moscow, Henry. *Russia Under the Czars*. New York: American Heritage, 1962.

Pavlov, Dmitri V. Trans. John Clinton Adams. *Leningrad 1941: The Blockade*. Chicago: The University of Chicago Press, 1965.

Salisbury, Harrison S. *The 900 Days: The Siege of Leningrad*. New York: Harper & Row, 1969.

Werth, Alexander. *Russia at War: 1941–1945*. New York: E. P. Dutton, 1964.

INDEX

★ ★ ★

Nazis, 11, 32, 35
Nazism, 28
Neva River, 13, 42
Nicholas II, 21
Nuremburg Trials, 33
Nurov, Captain Mikhail, 72

Pavlov, Dmitri V., 52, 55, 58, 74
Pearl Harbor, 44
People's Volunteers, 38
Peter the Great, 13-17, 24
Petrograd, 21, 24, 90
Piskarevsky Cemetery, 85
Poland, 23, 28, 31, 44
proletariat, 28

ration cards:
    forgery of, 52
    fraud and, 55
    generally, 52, 61
    murder for, 62
rationing, 49, 51
"Road of Life," 72, 74
Roosevelt, President Franklin D., 47
Russian Revolution, 18, 21

Savichev, Tanya, 9
Siege of Leningrad:
    animals, effect on, 56
    beginning of, 44
    birthrate during, 62
    censorship and, 86
    crime during, 62
    death tolls: 84; November-December 1941, 61; January 1942, 62
    disease during, 74
    end of, 82
    evacuation during, 77, 79
    flour consumption prior to, 73
    museum for, 89, 90
    second year of, 81
Shlisselburg, 43, 82
Shostakovich, Dmitry, 41, 82
Sky Day, 67
Soviet Union
    generally, 5, 21
    German invasion of, 35
    industry in, 27
Special Engine Column 48, 82
SS, 33
Stalingrad, 47, 79, 82

Stalin, Joseph:
    death of, 89
    dislike of Leningrad, 38
    generally, 24-28, 31, 32, 38, 44
    life under: pre-war, 24; post-war, 86
starvation, 44, 51, 58, 61, 79
Stepanov, Yuri, 7
St. Petersburg:
    after Russian Revolution, 21
    cultural life in, 18
    general, 13, 16, 90
    poverty in, 18

Treaty of Brest-Litovsk, 28
Trotsy, Leon, 21

United States (America), 44, 51

von Leeb, Field Marshal William Ritter, 36, 37, 42
Voroshilov, Kliment Y., 33, 44

Wehrmacht, 31-33, 82
"white nights," 33
Winter Palace, 16, 21, 89
"Winter War," 28
World War I, 21, 23
World War II, 5, 18, 32, 33, 47

Zhdanov, Andrey, 33, 38, 72
Zhukov, Georgy, 44